The Croc Does An Ironman

Steven Crenfeldt

Copyright © 2016 Steven Crenfeldt

All rights reserved. No part of the book may be transmitted or reproduced by any form or means, either mechanical or electronic, including recording and photocopying, or by any known storage and retrieval system, without permission in writing from the Publisher, except in the case of short quotations being used in a review.

National Library of Australia Cataloguing-in-Publication

Creator: Crenfeldt, Steven, 1976- author.

Title: The IronCroc does Busso / Steven Crenfeldt ; illustrated by Talisa Homer.

ISBN: 9780994477804 (paperback)

Target Audience: For primary school age.

Subjects: Crocodiles-Juvenile fiction.
        Ironman triathlons-Juvenile fiction.

Other Creators/Contributors: Homer, Talisa, illustrator.

Dewey Number: A823.4

For the virgins and repeaters, age-groupers and pros,

The Harry Hard-Cores and the Average Joes;

You are all equal at the end of the day;

Your times may be different, but the medal is the same.

Some just want to finish; others are chasing a spot

At the big dance in Kona, the home of the M-dot.

So swim like you're being chased and ride like you stole,

Run hard to the finish; it's time to Croc and roll!

It's the night before race day, and all through the house
Not a creature is stirring, not even a mouse.
The bikes have been hung in transition with care,
With hope that the tyres will remain filled with air.

The athletes are nestled all snug in their beds,
As visions of PBs dance in their heads.
Some are too restless to even count sheep,
While others have only just made it to sleep.

When from the alarm comes an ear-piercing chime,
They spring from their beds to check on the time.
After first breakfast, they're ready to rock;
It's still dark outside cos it's "Stupid O'clock!"

The moon brings faint lighting to the night sky
As all the first-timers begin questioning "Why?"
"Are they ready? Will they make it?
Can this thing be done?"
Then somebody whispers "Just go out and have fun!"

You've trained in the sunshine, the wind and the rain;
Your physio has fixed you, time and again.
You've tapered, you've stretched, you've carb-loaded too,
Done a few nervous wees and a big Number 2!

With bags packed and bike pump
you're soon out the door,

Excited and anxious of what is in store.

The silence is broken by speakers on stands

As the commentary team
shout out their commands.

"No bags in transition! Is your timing-band on?"
"Got a spare saddle? The pros have now gone!"
"Age-groupers leave in seventeen minutes!"
"Now head to the start-line...See you at the finish!"

The cannon then fires; you run and dive in!
Who made a washing-machine out of a swim?
You follow the buoys for 3.8 k
As the darkness above slowly turns into day.

It seems like forever you're away from dry land,
When all of a sudden your fingers touch sand.
Into transition, the chaos and stress;
The volunteers are waiting to help you get dressed.

Your bike's hanging out, just itching to ride,
Clip in at the mount line, then pedal with pride.
The bike is a buffet of food and drink;
Time to start eating; just do it, don't think!

Settle into your cadence, find rhythm and power;
Just keep those legs turning, regardless of hours.
Your bum hurts, your legs hurt, your shoulders hurt too;
You've tried to ride faster, but that's all you can do.

As you near the 180, start spinning those legs;
You'll be asking for more from those two little pegs.
Back to transition, the bike has been racked;
Now on with the runners, sunglasses and cap.

You know you can run, but today it's so hard;
You doubt you can make more than a few yards.
Crowds line the run course; they call out your name;
You manage a shuffle but you're in a world of pain.

42 k later, there's just metres to go;
You might have been flying or might have been slow.
But you've conquered the swim, you've conquered the ride,
You've conquered the run and have springs in your stride.

The cheer squad are screaming; they've been out there all day;
You throw out some *thank yous* and give them a wave.
The music is pumping; this crowd is not mild!
The party before you is getting quite wild.

The microphone's booming as you sprint down the chute;
You smile for the camera, but you just want to puke!
You've finished! You made it! You look up at the clock;
And hear the voice shout "You Are An IronCroc!"

Special thanks to the following businesses for helping to get our little project across the finish line:

When you're in Busselton for IMWA,
Stop by at these businesses and say G'day!
They're well worth the visit, while up and about,
So here's a shameless plug and a big shout out!

To the Tuff'n'Up Tri Squad, the ones wearing green;
If you're looking for a coach, then come join the team!
Rack your bike at Fat Duck Cycles and Espresso;
Enjoy a hot chocolate with extra marshmallows!

After your training, grab a meal at Dome,
To refuel yourself before you go home!
Bindi Nutrition is the only way
To give back to your body when smashing out Ks!

Physio SouthWest are the people to see
When you've got a pulled hamstring or a sore knee!
Viva Books help prepare for your taper
With something to read, like a reptilian caper!

The Croc appears courtesy of:
Tuff'n'Up Triathlon
Coaching – If you want to be seen,
you've got to wear green!

Leo & Finch appear courtesy of:
Local artist Talisa Homer

Guy and Kate from GK Endurance
Came on board early with just my assurance,
That we'd do their brand proud with a book that's quite cool;
A funny, yet helpful tri-training tool.

Thanks to you both; it's been loads of fun;
Stressful at times but we got the job done!
Whatever the weather; rain, hail or sun,
Keep an eye out for The Croc when you swim, ride and run!

Check out more of Talisa Homer's artwork at www.etsy.com/au/shop/leoandfinch and on Facebook. Orders can be made online or through the artist.

  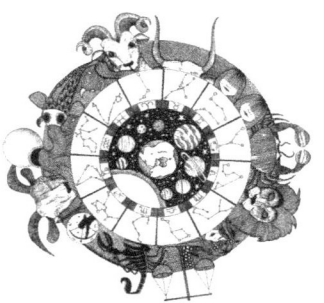

Steven Crenfeldt's first novel A Long Ride Back can be found on Facebook. Orders can be made through the author or at your local bookshop.

www.ingramcontent.com/pod-product-compliance
Lightning Source LLC
Chambersburg PA
CBHW040331300426
44113CB00020B/2725